Once I Carried Three Crows / Rachel Plummer

Once I Carried Three Crows

Rachel Plummer

Published in 2024 by Tapsalteerie
Tarland, Aberdeenshire
www.tapsalteerie.co.uk

Cover image: *Three Crows*, Henri Charles Guérard, Rijksmuseum

ISBN: 978-1-7384396-1-4

Printed and bound by Imprint Digital, UK

For Nana Jones and for Audrey,
at opposite ends of the dark telescope

Solar Eclipse

You slept late this morning
so I caught the eclipse for you
in a jam jar.

See how the glass contains it?

The wilting light over the garden,
the moon's perfect disc slipping
into place like a contact lens
on a wide open eye?

If you put your ear to the lid
you might hear birdsong
swell and then hush

or the cloud's tide-song rising
like sea-wrack.

Put the jar by your bedside,
let its dimness quiet
your early mornings.

Where Language Lives

One

Today I found the place where language lives.
It was between two cities, in the space
where weather tightens into sudden cold.
Your voice was nearly frozen, like a lamb
beneath its mother disappearing in
a snowblanked field. So almost-gone a thing
I thought that it might melt in my hot hand.
Your voice lived in that in-between lost land
and spoke to no one, though I heard it sing
a wordless song, as thin as frost is thin,
a sound that sank into the ground. I am
too used to cities, though, where all the old
earth's languages freeze fast in concrete ice
like grudges only silence can forgive.

Two

Sometimes I think I see it in the dark
beneath bridges. I think that it has wings
but cannot fly. It's shy; it can't be caught,
will surely die if caged or fade to air.
Perhaps it's only visible through glass:
a window. Mirror. Water gathered on
the ground between the tracks in this dark hall.
Perhaps I never saw it there at all.
The mind will trick itself like that, and one
winged thing can look much like another. Pass
from here into the light, and nothing's there.
Perhaps even the bridge was passing thought.
This is where language lives, among the things
that can't be seen or spoken, leave no mark.

Three

I searched for it in water, but the sea
has its own language, and the river too.
Even the old canal, which walks across
the city on a heron's legs, knows only
its own speech. The language of the drowning
is where water lives. Your voice knows this
and keeps away. It hides itself in trees
and in the shadows of the trees. It sees
the water rising to the sky like bliss
and wants to say, I too will soon be crowning
through the air to birth. It is lonely
up there in bare branches. It is like loss.
Or else it is like vanishing in blue
and finding speech where water used to be.

Four

Your language lives inside a melon seed.
I cut the mother melon open. In
the cavity are seeds like many tongues
and one is yours. Rain on the roof like seeds
and seeds pooled in the melon's bowl like rain.
We're here again; this place where language lives.
It's slippery as something newly birthed.
I plant it, though I know this salted earth
will never let it grow. The ground forgives
itself for offering no hope, while pain
grows here among the wild flowers and weeds
and needs no watering. The soil's black lungs
inflate and empty with a sound so thin
it could be speech bound by a melon seed.

Five

I hear you when the clouds speak rain to summer,
and summer with her uncleared throat of thunder
speaks through the sparking sap and sky to say
she will not step aside until she's done.
I hear you when the river starts to run
as if it's chased, and in the still before.
Speech is a form of water, always falling
seaward through the names its drains are calling.
The estuary mouths sonnets to the shore
in couplets, out and in, and nothing rhymes.
In times like these I miss the silent sun
who holds his tongue from day to quiet day.
His every breath's a tree to shelter under
while stormclouds speak an end to childhood's summer.

A Cluster of Mushrooms

Jelly Ear Fungus

Something is singing in the woods.

The trees listen to the hymn
of their own sap rising. It sounds like light.

Who is speaking secrets in the leafless places?

Who has longed to listen so fervently
that ears grew from the thick trunk of their body?

Who has heard the parable of the wild garlic?

Or waited not-alone in church with their knees too
far apart on the hassock, while a man presses
words into something else's ear?

Some secrets may be confessed

                    only to the trees.

He who has ears, let him hear.

St George's Mushroom

A blessing.
A blessing under the flowering garlic.
A congregation of little soapstone saints
suspended in the petrifying well of spring rain,
a palmful, a psalm, an offering.
Early to rise. A matins.

Pilgrim under fence posts, sleeping under
stars, eating the good, wet air,
turning up your bonemeal
face to the damp as the field is
turned by the plough before wheat,
scent of wheat in the rain,
field to flower to flour, hour on hour.

May will make a meal of you, pilgrim
The year swallows its first season whole.

Velvet Shank

rising from ash in the candlestump hours
late to the party, in last season's colours
she stands out in the cold waiting to be let in

fever-slick, starting to rust
an old fox fur fraying on her thin shoulders
one of those girls, you know
the ones, tongue in the snow
tasting long buried rot, she looks hungry
damn, she looks tired, hair not quite,
skin kind of clammy

don't let her in
through the door in the wall of the old year
where she comes scratching with all her fingers
until her long gloves are ragged
and the sound haunts the graves of the beech trees

don't let her tell you she's scared
to walk alone through the woods at night
in that frock (you know)
and her hair full of winter
and the night poured into a dirty glass, half drunk
and everyone else left hours ago

tomorrow the first light will find her
dragging herself home in a heavy, wet dress

Scarlet Elf Cup

I couldn't tell my mother
so I went to the woods and bled
into the cupped hands of a mushroom.

The blood in me loves falling
to leaf litter, feeding the earth
its own iron
    sip by sip by

Nothing is lost in the woods.
Even the smallest loss is gathered like dew
and swallowed.

I couldn't tell my mother
what the pale cups had caught,
how I knew my own blood
by its scent, how the ivy
couldn't cover it, how the cups
ran over with redness.

Sulphur Tuft

how much had you drunk that night
when you took the shortcut home through the woods
on migraine paths that can't bear streetlight
and heard the sporedust whispering

that safety exists
                    in numbers

and on broken limbs

they limned your path with phosphorescence
promised poison
in revenge for any man's harm
a fatal bite grown from the bark
saying don't walk home alone
after dark, after dark

Dead Man's Fingers

The man whose fingers grasp up from the ground
used to wait in the woods by the path with no name
to tell women walking by themselves in the low sun
what he thought of their clothing, weight or skin,
their smile,
how their smartphones were terrible burdens,
that they really should live in the moment,
of the suitability of their shoes for the weather,
and the way they wore their hair, what it meant,
the language he believed they spoke,
their hijab their bindi their crucifix
how much prettier they would look if,
and what they really ought to remember,
on whether they were married,
or walked a dog,
or seemed frightened
and, above all, how cruel the women were,
every one of them, how desperately cruel
to not welcome his opinions, to hurry homewards
with eyes on the tree roots, to not see
what a good man he was.

See how blackened and bulbous the fingers?

I won't tell you how he died.

Purple Brittlegill

As a bird mother eating and vomiting
she swallows down every morsel and boaks
it into the hungry mouths of the forest.

There is now no time to remember
how beautiful she was, how her skin was dark
and smooth as a new conker.

Not while her children are needing
and needing
and flesh bitten down
to the bone white
pokes from the moth eaten scraps of her
old satin gown.

Yellow Stainer

Ever taken your witch to the woods
                 full bladdered
and made her squat,

returned in a month to find a spill
of mushrooms, pale topped and pink
underbellied, folds of soft pink
to put your pink fingers in, to fill, to know
like the wasp knows
the stamen, its dust of yellow
pollen, the way the mushroom will lift its yellow skirt
at the sight of you, the way it will,
when pink finger-nailed, let go
of all the yellow it has held
until it can't be kept inside?

Sickening, sickening,
                but only to some.

Giant Polypore

A generous body, wide set, spilling out of herself,
dimpled in the sun, thickly fleshed, thick,
wrapping her thighs around the base of the beech trunk,
layered like pastry, like curls of new butter, spread,
puffed, gorged on stump and root and rain, rolling
in it, swollen with it, solid as a second helping,
third, fourth, growing forth, growing strong, growing
heavy and unshakeable as the dirt, ample,
a big girl, giantess, unafraid
     to fill up
        her space.

Uncut

In dark corners the hair grows through my skin
as dense as ivy through old brick, soil-dank
and root-tangled, earthy as stamen, frank
against a sun-starved ground stretched thin:
moonwhite. Fishwhite. Almost alive within.
Because I love wild flowers, and the blank
spaces in buildings gone to wreck, the rank
water in ponds now stagnant, toothless grin
of broken glass and empty window pane
that crumble the respectable edges,
I let it grow. Let's bring the hidden, shy
things to the air. Let's not be so mundane
we miss what freedom wilderness pledges
to hairy, rain-drunk earth; to endless sky.

Pentad

One

Two nights to swallow the Atlantic ocean
mouthful by icy mouthful,
until our bellies swelled with salt.

I remember the way she shimmy-shimmied like a comet
slipping the earth's slinky atmosphere from its shoulders,
the little bitter handfuls of her breasts,

my tongue on her skin's DNA, the taste of its helix,
the taste of her dragon ink, coyote spill, her eyeshine.

Two

She was silent and squid silver,
brought up from a sea trench
into surface pressure so low she might at any moment disperse
through the atmosphere, coalesce
into satellite, a moon cradled in orbit.

She moonsang and moondanced, she spoke in moonvoices,
she held the moon in her eye water

my touch left indelible marks in the dust of her craters.

Three

Her body spanned a bed as if bridging
two shores. I covered her eyes and her penis,
the criss-cross of her wrists.

The air grew hot and melted in puddles on her rib scars.

Her mouth was a velvet bow;
I took one end of its ribbon and pulled the tight knot open.

Four

When she released my vulva from her birdcage hands

we went out and swam lengths of the dark city market,
strawberries and cardamom crackling their static
on our acetate tongues, weighed down with the light
that tumbled after us from the sleepless white bed.

Our fingers touched, wet with strawberry, red and wet
with their spiced, fragrant juices.

Five

Her voice fell like leaves from our window
green in the monochrome night.

I wanted to hold the glint of her sea glass eyes
in a pair of tongs, to fan out their irradiated atoms
like a tarot deck on a transparent slide.

I remember her voice, her clenched vowels turning in place
with a pulsar's rapid blink, the starmap of her abdomen

the patina of her touch on my skin's copper surface.

The Worm

The worm eats memories.
She has specific tastes;
prefers them cool, eases
them down with half a glass
of iced Chianti. Faced
with anything flesh-hot
she can't help but recoil.
She wants them raw. Ripe as
oysters that slip down oil
sleek to the tightened knot
of her stomach and work
it open. Best of all
are old ones that have grown
solid; hard as a fist
in her soft throat. She sucks
them small, the layered schist
eroding into small
mouthfuls of soft sandstone.

So few are brave enough
to reach into her fat
belly and pull out tough
strands of undigested
rememberings. You might
lose fingers. Might find all
your lost thoughts are already
topsoil. Let them go
unchallenged, uncontested
into the ground at night
like worms from frost. Let them
be lost. You cannot see
things as the blind mind-worm
can see. You are confused.
And now someone you used
to know comes near to say
'Do you remember when.'
But *when* has been eaten.

Fare

It's true what they say: we always have the best stories.

Like the time Aethelfrith, the pagan king,
climbed into my cab and commanded me to drive
back and forth over the Tyne, searching for his lost brother.
No reasoning with him.
He wound the window down
as if the glass itself was an obstruction.

Grief will do that to you. It runs through the body
black and hard as a coal seam.

Once I carried three crows through Leaves Park
to Spital Tongues, where they got out and collected souls
in the boot of my car.
We drove clear of the city to the Brig o' Dread
which rose huge as a thunderous sky
over the land between the living and the dead.

Oftentimes it's advice they're really wanting.
You can tell certain things to the back of a man's head
that you wouldn't say to his face.

Hadrian's Wall wanted me to carry him
the breadth of the land, to the Solway Firth.
Packed himself brick by brick into the back of my cab,
the meter already ticking like woodlice.
I said you can only spread yourself so wide.
So thin.

My favourite? Has to be the Tyne herself.
Classy lady. Grey haired, carrying everything.
She spoke with the soft voice of water.
I wanted to keep her
there on the back seat forever, the last fare
I'd ever carry. But she was bound for the coast
where the North Sea waited to meet her.
Stay, I started to say, but in the rearview mirror
I saw she was already tide

going out, and in, and out again.

Wide as the Ocean is

I love you as the North Sea loves a boat
when bearing it high up onto the shore,
or as a piece of driftwood loves to float
in with the tide to Gullane. I adore
you as the Firth of Forth adores the train,
its track, the bridge it crosses over and
the bridge's black reflection in the rain
bloated river. I love you like the land
can't help loving the coast and breaks itself
apart to let the ocean in, and like
a dizzy, new-formed cyclone loves the Gulf
Stream, like storm water loves a lightning strike.
I love you as a drowned man loves the sea;
I am the boat that begs you shipwreck me.

Delilah

I'll braid your hair into
a rope, my love, a rope
to moor you to my shore

as if you were a blue
boat on a black sea. Hope
will keep you floating, pour

you out into a glass
bottle to balance on
my bedside table. There

I'll keep your lips, your brass
teeth and your neck, your swan
stark neck, my love, your hair-

rope noosed around it like
a hangman's necklace. See
right here, the place that length

of conger black could strike
your unmarred back for me
and leave it bruised. Such strength

contained within the braid
that binds your bed to mine.
Such longing to be freed,

such life, that if I made
a knife and cut that twine
I swear your hair would bleed.

The Iron Children

Along our street the iron children come,
cast and wrought. The road rings like a struck
cymbal below their clanging feet. For luck
we clank our coins into their mouths, all dumb
as metal, hear them rattle down and thrum
the stainless engines deep inside each quick
gullet. They flood the street with blood-smell, thick
as rust; church bell faces. What will become
of the mother carrying her iron child
inside of her, a silver pear to weigh
her down? Pot-bellied, saucepan-bellied. Thirsting
for the iron monger's ore, her child
hungry. Its metal, melted down, would pay
a heavy debt, or fill a womb to bursting.

Houses

One

We grew up in a funhouse. The envy
of other children; we bloodied our noses
on the false walls, spent eighteen years
lost in the mirror maze.

The funhouse mirrors distorted us, bodies
stretched or pressed, obese, too short.
Boneless. Faceless. Smur of breath
on the curved quicksilver surfaces.

Watched, we drew our smiles like thread
through a needle eye, we drew them
in grease paint. Clown smiles, wide
in the strobe light. An optical illusion.

Soon the bulbs began to fade. The paint
to curl like pencil shavings. The moving
floor to judder as if it struggled
for breath. By the time we left

the funhouse we were seasick on solid
ground, unused to the earth's firmness
under our feet, blinded by the day's
true light. Out of place. Almost homesick.

Two

Once our house was loud with birdwings. House
martin, coal tit. Feathers beating the close wooden walls.

Later our house was an abandoned nest box
incubating egg shells, dead leaves, three naked helpless

nuthatch chicks rooting for beech mast, maggots in the nest
bed. The birdhouse stank of wood rot and rotting

bird bones, sternum and scapula. We stripped them, starving
for the leather-scrapes of tendon that still clung in strings.

Empty. Stomachs clenched tight as fists. And we
were birds, air-light and perching, finally hollow

enough to dart from the door's black eye to the white eye
of the sun, blinding and new over the garden.

Three

One doll turned in place to the imagined song
of a music box. One sat at a miniature table
mouthing daintily at her ceramic meal. The last
stood motionless by the dollhouse door, jointed limbs
stiffly poised. Each a perfect porcelain Goldilocks.

The dollmaker's voice was bear growl
through the glassless windows. The dollmother
picked apart elbows, pried painted glass eyes
from their sockets, stuffed bellies with cotton.
She posed the dolls on metal stands.

At night the three dolls drew their floral curtains
tight and sucked at bonbons. The dollhouse filled
with the stretch of hollow mouths, the weighted blink
of horsehair eyelashes. Each morning the dollmaker
stripped them to see if they were bleeding yet.

Four

When the sea is white against the rock, the tower
white above the rock, when the lantern spins
like a coin over the rough tide's flood
or ebb, then the lighthouse keeper emerges.

Her footsteps are heard on the staircase: the tick
of a grandfather clock, the paced sway of
its pendulum. The lighthouse keeper
doesn't hurry to the lamp room

to tend the waiting beam. She lets the light's
edges fray to moth-wings over the water,
the lamp's full circle wane to a crescent
before she reaches the solitary watch.

Below her is white sea, the black weed stirred
to the surface, the tower's anchor dropped
into the outcrop. Across the sea no ships, only
the fireflies of other lighthouses signalling their distress.

Five

These are the nights I strap myself in
to the ghost train. The ghost walls are papered
with photographs and white ribbons hang

from the ceiling like hair.
I tour the rooms, greet their inhabitants,
note each new absence. The skeleton

driver creeps between the empty
carriages, she strokes my cheek,
fills my ears with wet soil.

Now at moonrise the house's marrow
tightens in its husk. The train stops suddenly.
Ghosts crowd the windows,

humming like crickets in the dead garden
watching every departure

A Wedding

Fire is an act of naming
and renaming. Like many men, fire loves
destructively. A vanity. I love you
but I'd love you more if you had all the properties of me:

My heat. My height. My colour. My propensity
to ash. Intensity that's pale, or even white.

Love at first light.
The first light man-made (dangerous).
This is how fire loves you.
You ember-silk, you coal-smoke-veil, you choking.

Give yourself away.
Let lace melt to your face and call it passion.
Let all who love you gather
at the crematorium to sing

here comes the bride to singe a ring in skin,
to burn away her old name.

Espousal

The Woman who Married the North Sea

You know what they say about older men.
Experienced.
He was a Viking; bold, black
as an eel. He'd been around, been intimate
with the land's soft edges,
dipped his cold tongue into the Skagerrak.

He brought me trinkets:
jellyfish scattered like spilled pennies
on the beach at Portobello,
delicately weed-wrapped plastic bags,
the rotting carcass of a sperm whale, his foam
white beard to caress my toes.

On our wedding night
the spray was thick as ambergris, the sand
fragile with worm casts.
I kissed his silvery pout.
Across the sea the moon sank
bright as a wrasse at the Rhine's mouth.

The Woman who Married the Eiffel Tower

I always liked them tall.
When I first saw him, I found his neck
arched like a peacock displaying itself.
I stood beneath his bulk, his balustrades blank
against the puddled iron sky.

I knew, right then, that I wanted to taste
his framework, my tongue to his struts. Shameless.
I wanted to inhale
through spaces in his endless lattice.

The next day I went up inside him.
I felt how he dwarfed me, his amusement
at my insignificance, my warmth
nothing like the sun that made him sway
over days as if dancing.
When I touched him, my name
was a vibration in his structure.
It ached like a tooth.

We married in the spring under a thousand watt moon.
He was an arc; exponential, neon
bulbs like blinking eyes.
Against my ear I heard the sound he made while cooling,
the twang of his wires, his stretched cartilage.

I kissed his mouth, my husband, the memory
of the night we met electric in my mind –
how I stood at the window of a hotel room
on the Rue Augereau and watched him lensed
against the distant stars, a bowstring
spanning the dim city below. That night I dreamed
that one day I might take his name,
his shape.

The Woman who Married Sonic the Hedgehog

Love's not a race
they say, and though
at first you rushed
through me like Concorde
it took ten years
to get from there to a ring.

Look
I'm a quick
learner and you see patterns
in the atoms
of a PC screen but
love's chaos.

Love's a daily restart.
Love leaves you
crushed. Transformed. Blue.
Love lumbers
slow as memory
impossible to outpace.

The Woman who Married Luigi

You weren't the obvious choice;
muted
not like your brother, who was
red-breasted
as a coca-cola Santa.

You were green.
Tall and slender
as a poplar.

Your leaps
ungainly, shy,
a moustachioed Bambi
all knee
all prominent rib.

You caught my eye like a feather
from the air.

You grew to twice
your former size
under my hot-water gaze.

Little brother.

Your plumber's hands
your handful of wrench
your eyes
our love
mushrooming in the shadow.

The Woman who Married a Lego Man

I fell in love at six years old
and knew it was forever. Back then we were both new,
shiny from the box. I admired the plastic
up-turned egg-cup of his hair, the way it cradled
his cylindrical head like the palm of a hand.

People told me to move on to bigger things
but I loved the way he fit in my fingers.
I built us a succession of square homes,
mismatched bricks on a sheet of lurid grass,
my man stood by the French windows
beckoning.

As I grew, I grew
to appreciate other things;
his androgyny, the cubic smoothness where his genitals
should have been. I liked his habit
of keeping quiet, his manly stoicism, his small fists
endlessly offering.

How many women are lucky enough
to marry their childhood sweetheart?
I tell them, 'he keeps me young'.
I say I like them poseable. Stiff
upper lipped. A possession.

SpOuse

She should have died a spinster.
A hag, like when I found her
hermiting below sea level, unwashed,
her hair full of birds.

She should've stayed stagnant,
heavy with marsh and Ouse. Her tadpole
tongue, her moss, her mouthful of frog.
Her pale skin bog-preserved, expansive.

Oh I won't deny that drained, dredged,
she cleaned up well. That on our wedding day
I saw the horizon in her mud-green eyes
and wanted to flood her
with new beginnings, homes, roads; to populate
her hidden spaces, to open her.

But I think back on her meres,
her veil of damp willow,
and feel the loss
of all those sunken acres. Her
saltwater hollows. The way she came to me,
a sedge warbler in her cupped hands.

My Father's Heart

So I tell myself we need to sit down
and talk it out: just me, my dad and
his heart problems.

And isn't that a bold metaphor.
Hasn't he always had *heart problems*.

Kept too much locked up too tight,
let that life-muscle atrophy.

Let veins clog like drains full of storm-wrack
for blood no thicker than flood
water, let arteries close like hands
into fists I think

we must sit down together,
me and my father's heart,
and shake hands like strangers.

I'll tilt my head to appear sympathetic and he'll tell me
he's getting older and wants to make amends.

Perhaps I'll take out my strong needle
and mend him like a shoe, teach him how to be sturdy
like a woman's heart, like a girl's.

I'll teach him how to bleed, how to let blood go
and not grieve it.

I'll teach him how to take
blood blue and leave it
red, how to hammer at a man's chest
until he hears you.

Perhaps I'll hold him, my father's heart,
hold him cupped in my hands like a too-soon baby
and sing him quiet like a surgeon wouldn't.

Perhaps I'll give him the things he couldn't
give us, give like I've got it to spare.
Perhaps we'll sit there: me,
my dad, and his tentacle tangle of
coronary arteries trailing their tails on
the floor I've just mopped, and have tea.

Perhaps we'll talk. Perhaps we'll open
up like veins for statins, and we'll promise
to ring more often, be bells for matins, chime.

I tell myself he'll show this time.

The Mermaid

In the communal garden
where my daughter plays
I look for needles:
used, lurking
sharp as the mouths of tiny snakes
ready to snag her ankles. Such
were the mermaid's teeth.

Or they were like the splintered bones
of fish, the flesh
still clinging grey
or pink in flakes
that looked like they would itch
the exposed gums, catch
in the throat.

Animal. Broad
and final, the thick arms
of a debt collector.
She was the sea rock
at Gullane, the mossed rock
wall, she was
the North Sea's boundary.

I saw her squat in the sand
that morning, solid
as a housing estate. My daughter
bright as a coin
barefoot by her rock pool, the water
catching at the shore's
pale ankles.

The tide rang like a bell
chiming the creature out
into the Forth's cradle,
its jellyfish forest of floating plastic bags.
My daughter
knee deep in the swell
stared out as if into traffic.

On the public beach
where my daughter plays
I look for teeth,
mermaid-rare
in the loose sand,
their needle points worn jagged
as a sea arch.

Yellow

Once, at the end of a long road
I met a man who claimed to be my father.
Taking my hand, he led me to a field of sunflowers:
the world's end.

Such bright blooms! Such fire
at the world's end! Such wings! Such mouths,
opening to eat the light from the air,
such a wideness of yellow.

'Father,' I said, and the man who
claimed to be my father took the word from my tongue
and buried it. Out of the soil
a hummingbird grew.

Iris

The Strongest Granny in the World

Iris can power-lift the Thames.
The trick, she says, is all in the balance. The way she shifts
her centre of gravity to accommodate the water's flowing.

Iris holds the Mississippi in her firm grip,
heaves the Nile up onto her chest,
lifts the Rhine over her head for a slow count of three.

She is deceptively small. Thin wrists. Her fists
fit within her husband's like a conker in its green shell.
She carries him, bridal-style, through wetlands.

Under the championship lights the other grannies fall away
one by one, until Iris is left alone to kiss the Orinoco
and hold it up to the roaring crowd.

When asked, she tells them training is vital.
Each week she finds local streams to pry up from the land,
to shoulder, until her steel hair dampens.

She says all water longs to return to the air.

That rain will raise itself up like the generations.
That even the Amazon, goddess of all rivers, is only vapour
strengthening itself for ascension.

The Oldest Particle Physicist at CERN

In one direction, she releases an albatross.
In the other, a vulture.
They plunge through the pipes like light.

Here, the wing meets no resistance
to its lust for acceleration.
Momentum is angular.

Deep underground Iris leans on the laws
she's defying. Her bones
are hollowing,

small tunnels in the dark
where the God of Almost-Nothing could crack
his soft shell open.

The circle floods with flight.
The miles-wide circle with its cargo of feathers.
The birds collide

head-on, and split
into a flock of gannets, hungry, crying
out at the shock of existence.

Iris weeps.
There's nothing like speed
to reveal what you're made of,

she says, but finds speech
falling from her like gravity.
Strange. She spreads herself wide as a wing.

She's itching to rise.
She's made for collision.
Iris bursts through the Earth like birdsong.

The Oldest Porn Star in the World

Iris makes love to the camera – cool glass warming
to her heat, shutter clacking at her touch
like the spines of a poisonous fish.

She caresses it. Licks the lens; she wants it wet.
Give it to me darling
she says, and her vulva is a darkroom,
baths of acetic acid and the intimate smell of ammonia.
She lets it all show. The sleepy sag of her labia, clitoris
new-butterfly textured,
wet winged and slow to unfurl in the studio light.

The camera is a candid lover. The camera loves her
milky eyes, the rotten pears of her breasts:
hairy-nippled, hanging like empty promises.

All she cares for, she says, is the click
in the dark like the wink of an eye. The way orgasm comes
in a flash, and illuminates everything.

Robogranny

Flesh is a burden. Iris remembers
how it started, the transition from granny to robot
granny, how incrementally her flesh
fell away from her: how first the knee
gave up its bone, then the rest of the body,
jealous, traded itself in for chrome.

She remembers the lungs
pushing at the bars of their cage,
the heart raging at its red tide,
the eyes with their light, the tight
grip of the hip to each socketed thigh.

Her soul, shy, hides in the solder,
tacking the brain's electronics
to its circuit board.

Iris takes all her faith and seals it in a wire.

She locks it behind a logic gate and says
let it be stored here like memory, in zeros and ones.

Iris knows the taste of metal.
She knows it like she knew the push
from womb to air, once; the spark
of charge on the bare places inside her.

That weak flesh has been upgraded
to something that will not rot.
Weightless as current. An unburdening.

Spidergranny

Her lycra suit sags like a pair of old tights.
Still, Iris slips it on each night
when small shadows begin to pool into night-tide

and every corner of the house
holds signs of struggle. Somewhere out
in the city, a granddaughter shouts.

Iris springs from the window.
She webs through streets she has always known;
masked, leaving traces snatched on lampposts.

No man who lifts a hand to her offspring
is safe from her. No man is safe
while Iris swings through the city on silk,

the wolf spider, widow, the redback
grown hungry for harm. The black
hairs on her abdomen are slick

with irritant. They quiver.
Iris's fangs flood with venom, that liquid shiver.
Soon she will wrap her enemies in silver

and tuck them away into corners.
There are so many granddaughters.
Children of the egg, and of the egg's egg. Hers.

Their own. No man's. She says
she would climb walls for those girls. By day
she knits a white lace

web to wrap her newest grandchild in. She waits
for the mother to swell, to make herself a safe place
and lay.

The Biggest Granny in the World

This is what happens on an island.
With nothing to hunt them, grannies grow.

Iris turns her broad back to the wind
and other grannies shelter in the lee of her body.
She wades hip-deep in the North Sea
plucking posies of orcas from the water
and her feet flatten the seabed.

Her spine is the line of extinct volcanoes
at the drifted edge of tectonic plates.
Snow-capped. Heat-tapped.
Her blood is sap in the trunks of her veins.
Her brains are tornado.
Her heart is an island in a red sea.

Fisherman, fisherman,
stay away, be afraid of the island
where the giant grannies beat their naked chests
and sing with the voice of the whirlpool.

Their fires can be seen from the mainland,
burnt offerings to the goddess of small things
grown wild, to the mother of land
risen up from the sea, to the spaewife, with-woman, witch,
the hag.

The Oldest Optician in the World

This is the eye
of a storm. Something wide open.
This is the neverblink
with the long tornado of its pupil
sucking the sky in, collapsing
the roof of the world into sinkhole.

This is the eyewall.
This is where air turns
to stone. This is the still place.
You know it like a lens knows
the eye. The iris.

Iris is almost gone
from the world, there's nothing left of her
but cyclone, and she's circling
the place where the air sank.

Iris is a storm-chaser,
her voice is hurricane,
she lives in the pinhole
light of the storm-
pause. Clouds spiral in her eyes.

The First Granny in Space

Gravity casts her off like a lace shawl.

Movement is easier here, but it's lonely
out under the earthrise. The eyes
of satellites wink as she drifts out of atmosphere's reach
heading out to the heat at the start of it all,
the static rush and recede.

Iris radioes back to Ground Control,
she says age is just distance
from home. That the ground must give up
its hold on each of us sooner or later.

Earth lets her go. Earth knows the sun;
the taut and slack of stars, and what it is
to need space.

It's a solo trip.

Many wanted to come
but none quite hit the mark. None loved as she loved
the ellipse in the dark, the spark, the heart
in its decaying orbit: pulse –

pulse, each pause between the beats
a new eclipse.

Out here life is nothing but light.

Iris thinks she might never come back.
She heads for the black, while somewhere below
her granddaughter kisses the eye of a telescope.

The Oldest Stripper in the World

Iris takes off the dress she was buried in.
Under it, her skin
has become a new dress, hung from thin

wire shoulders. This, she removes.
Lets fall. How new
she is, beneath, how ancient blue

her veins, their lace over the muscle.
These are harder to detach. A tangle
her skinned fingers struggle

to remove. Once muscle-stripped
and bare, the softness of organs is tipped
from the rib-vase, the jug of her hips.

Her audience is warming to the show.
They want to tuck their silver into bones
before they're gone. They know

the body's knack for fading, and how fast
a life's undone. The hair, the voice, that taste
of carbon lingering in air. It cannot last.

Betty's House

The fire is bright as tinfoil in the grate
at Betty Jones's house this time of year
and kitchen steam mirrors the fog, a sheer
silk scarf draped round the copse's neck, ornate
as rooks. The days collapse under the weight
of winter's darkening; another year
reflected in each bauble's glassy sphere
and hung to catch the fire's guttering light.

Bring to this house your songs and silences.

Leave all the old year's disappointments by
the old coal bin and come inside. The slow
years pass but Betty's house remains; fences
us in beneath a hard December sky
that whitens with what might be ash, or snow.

Sonnet for A.

I dreamed one night you turned into a crow
and wouldn't leave my rooftop night or day
but hid flight's feathered secret fast away
and scraped the chimneys with your voice's bow.

I listened from the lonely room below
and heard the words your music could not say
(as nothing speaks in crowlight but to pray
and nothing stays that has the power to go).

So hours fall without you like black snow
in coal drifts, hiding each familiar way
and covering the rooftops with a spray
of darkness deeper than feathers could know.

I dream of you at dawn when crows are crying
and hope that, though we're parted, you are flying.

Acknowledgements

With thanks to the editors of the following publications, in which versions of some of these poems have previously appeared: Agenda, Sogo magazine, The Dark Horse, *Fourteen Poems to Say I Love You* from Candlestick Press, the anthology *154* from Live Canon, And Other Poems, The Emma Press *Anthology of Love*, The Fenland Reed, Mslexia, Shoreline of Infinity, The Scottish Book Trust New Writing Awards Sampler 2016, *We Were Always Here*, *A Queer Words Anthology* from 404Ink, The Queen's Head, The Stinging Fly, and The Flambard Prize.

I owe much to the wonderful people at Scottish Book Trust for my 2016 New Writers Award for Poetry, and for their unwavering support over the years since. I'm grateful to my New Writers Award mentor Gerry Cambridge, whose insight helped to shape many of these poems.

Many thanks to Dave Coates, whose thoughtful editing of this collection has made it what it is, and to dear friend and comrade Rosamund Taylor, whose opinion of my poems will always be the first I look for.

I will always be grateful to my earliest mentors, Stuart Henson and John Greening, for encouraging a love of poetry in me from childhood and supporting me and my work to this day.

My thanks to poetry pals Alice Tarbuck, Annie Rutherford, Russell Jones, Andrew Blair and Ross McCleary, whose friendship, support and relentless shenanigans have all contributed to my ability, practically or psychologically, to write this book.

And a huge thank you to Duncan of Tapsalteerie, for believing in this collection enough to offer it a home, and for the benefit of an enviable eye for detail combined with a genuine care for poetry and the arts.

Finally, my gratitude always to my wonderful family, whose love for and faith in me is behind anything I might ever accomplish.

www.tapsalteerie.co.uk

Tapsalteerie is an award-winning poetry publishing house based in rural Aberdeenshire. We produce an eclectic range of publications with a focus on new poets, translation, collaborations and innovative writing.